Outlying Districts

Books by Anselm Hollo

Translations

Outlying Districts

POEMS BY ANSELM HOLLO

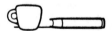

COFFEE HOUSE PRESS :: MINNEAPOLIS :: 1990

Some of these poems first appeared, many in earlier versions, in the following magazines: *Abraxas, Aileron, And, Avec, Blind Date, Bombay Gin, Brief, Carbuncle, c/o, Continental Drifter, Cover Arts New York, Exquisite Corpse, Falk, Fell Swoop: The All-Bohemian Review, Giants Play Well in the Drizzle, Human Means, Infolio, In This Corner, mini, New American Writing, New Delta Review, notus, Open 24 Hours, Pacific Review, Poetry Flash, Pome, Puerto del Sol, Rolling Stock, Screens & Tasted Parallels, See and Spell, Shock's Bridge, Talus, Taos Review, Teachers & Writers, The Pearl, The Worm in the Rain, This Is Important, Tom Clark Editions, Tortilla, Transfer, West Coast Review,* and *Zajets.*

A number of poems were published in chapbooks by Smithereens Press (*Outlying Districts*) and Fell Swoop (*Minigolf*).

The publisher thanks the following organizations whose support helped make this book possible: The National Endowment for the Arts, a federal agency; Dayton Hudson Foundation; Cowles Media/Star Tribune; Minnesota State Arts Board; Northwest Area Foundation; and United Arts.

Coffee House Press books are distributed to trade by CONSORTIUM BOOK SALES AND DISTRIBUTION, 287 East Sixth Street, Suite 365, Saint Paul, Minnesota 55101. Our books are also available through all major library distributors and jobbers, and through most small press distributors, including Bookpeople, Bookslinger, Inland, Pacific Pipeline, and Small Press Distribution. For personal orders, catalogs or other information, write to:
COFFEE HOUSE PRESS
27 NORTH FOURTH STREET, SUITE 400, MINNEAPOLIS, MN 55401.

Library of Congress Cataloging in Publication Data
Hollo, Anselm
    Outlying Districts : poems / by Anselm Hollo
        p. cm.
    ISBN 0-918273-76-5 : $8.95
    I. Title
PR6015.0415098 1990   90-35355
821'.914--dc20   CIP-

Contents

Minigolf

The Dada Letter

Arcana Gardens

For Jane

from her querimonious querido

Outlying Districts

Holliday, Dr. John Henry, 86 – 7, 150
Hollo, Anselm, 189
"Home on the Range," 175

— From the Index to *Great Plains*
by Ian Frazier (New York, 1989, FSG)

Things to Do at
453 South 1300 East,
Winter '86

Read ten thousand lines
by the poets of Finland

translate two hundred and twenty-six

then sit & stare
across to where sky meets dead sea
out beyond the polis
of this valley

Think of "SIERRA PLUG, the *Ecological* Chaw"

see hundreds of erstwhile
(*very* erstwhile) trees go up in smog
from the assholes of fast little vehicles

get up and eat some fast little vehicle

That mixed choir's really raving away on the radio

Now contemplate the wish baskets in the Xmas tree
slow down past the speed of light

see them go up & down up & down
floating across the desert & over the mountains

Feel gentleness invade you with the thought of her
who brought you here

& here she is   no need to write now

diary

One day's
big event was when

the cardboard
box I had set on

top of logs burning
in the grate toppled out

of the fireplace in a lively
state of combustion

viento

Big Wind
BANGS
against shoebox house

Down in Santa Fe Phil Whalen tells us
          Duerden couldn't *stand* it

yet it is what goes
every second,
through each one of our cells

blowing each instant through every thing
& every thing through each instant

slow through rocks,
                    fast through the protein

even faster through the medium called "air"
which lives above "water" a medium with "earth" in it

upon which stands our house
using both "water" & "air"
day & night, adding "fire"

in the form of candles, kerosene stove,
& just the way we look

fast through the protein,
                    slow through rocks

certainly using itself to the max every second, no?

Yet, surely this is a place
quite marked by our little quirks

one of which, "love": an intangible tango

local color

Another plane staggers in.
And there, in the middle distance,

the dirigible *Mark Strand*.
Its captain seems to be waving.

Up here on the mountaintop
everything looks just hunky-dory.

It'll all be gone
in a blink of your eye.

It will be followed by
Jefferson and / or Donald Duck.

"Dig yields wealth of knowledge
on Utah's ancients"

Aahh, the ancients, the lovely ancients

they lived in villages
they made handsome pots
they salted the deer
(plenty of salt around here)

they strode in & out of their heads
all over these hills

they raised the young
humored the old
buried the dead
& kept out the cold

They were terrific!
unlike present millions
of even more clever-brained
forked bags of water

now zapping by in their steel
& plastic shells
out there

And that was Mr Cheapo Nostalgia speaking

though sentiment
                    swings either way:

good luck to the living

direct address

Bright sun   double yellow
line down the middle   a red one
on the far curbside   drums on the radio

Man in too short check pants glides by like daffodil
& I sit here thinking the Vice President
then thinking the Vice President
needs a new job & a bandido moustache

Who's speaking   "The Finnish-American Poet?"
no no   the poet of the precise non sequitur
in his middle years
in the days of The Great Condom Revival

Hello how are ya   ça va, ça va
*Every*body's a genius at least once a year

0600 hrs / *for Simon Pettet*
shamelessly cannibalizing his versions
of the French Romantics

In the middle of the party
                    balancing her purse
      on classical leg . . . fried . . .
                            Be always
my queen, star-studded . . . my face, still red
            in the black grapes . . . your dainty
      foot in the trellis . . .
"Tie him up while I slip into something becoming"
      Moaned
under those heavy rocks, Eskimo
            for some few moments more
in the multinational record company offices
WAKE UP! O lake! O silent rocks! O caves! Dark
forest! Let it be! Let it be! I rise! I fall
in the lake! and the skies are screaming
under the scarf of Iris
and a dignified fellow in two-tone suede hat passes
on his way to the Chinese collection, like clockwork

the phone

"Hi! My name is Scott Cary. I just bought *Up Late*
and read your poems in it
and read in the notes that you live
in Salt Lake City. So I wanted to tell you I think
you're really a good poet."

"Well, thank you. (Pause.) Did you enjoy
the rest of the anthology?"

"Well, I just got it. (Pause.) I'm sitting here reading it
in a restaurant."

"I see." (Pause.)

"Well — what do you do for money?"

(Pause.) "That's — *my* business, isn't it?"

"Hee-hee . . . (Pause.) Well, maybe see you around."

"Take it easy."

A little later,

THE DOOR:

"Hi! My name is
Casanova
Hamilton.
What's yours?"

"No
Sale."

— time to hit the streets for a spell —

Pocatello, Idaho

thin man whacking

away at tire with mattock

in 7-11 parking lot

9 p.m.

Saturday night

we
saw
that
sight

feeling somewhat lost,
like any "old wisdom"

lost with the wisdom like grizzled
old rider of motorbike
parked
by the side of Wyoming road

has he taken his wisdom on a final hike
across that scrubby *melancholia?*

saw him stuff eggs of hen & bits of pig
into still handsome face
at the truck stop only minutes ago
& now he's gone

there stands
his chopper
monument

well he's probably just taking a shit
he'll be back & pass you at eighty-five miles an hour
old wisdom intact

In this court of entrance stood
the gigantic remains
of a supposition…

Where the sun sets on the purple sage
the buffalo roam no more, no more

& the cowboy poet is mostly a crashing bore
& the state's economy is up Shitski Prospekt

the great god Morton Thiokol belches
with the great god Moroni
after the meal they've made of Ute & Shoshoni

& any human being of finer sensibilities

(an "intellectual"
of sorts & a city boy
even though you've spent
much of your grown-up life
in small country towns
you're still grateful
even amazed that these People of the Country
don't gang up on you & kill you

— NASO

anti-lullaby

Wake up from a dream
of a large herd (very verbal)
of porcine politicos

assembled for imminent charge off cliff

Well, that's . . . that's almost interesting

The sun also has risen
& we better get on with it

"early in de mawnin' an de road is gettin' light"

So let's tango on down
        the shining path
to breakfast
        at the Café Spartacus

so there's this little man

down the street "little"
in that he ain't "big"
has an argument with his woman
gets his gun

a little .22-caliber gun
& hops in the truck
his wife calls the cops afraid
he'll hurt himself

so they give chase
& corner him up a canyon
he's still upset he points
the gun at his head

he doesn't speak the lingo too well
he waves his arms & another
little man in a uniform
shoots him dead

(then there's the other kind
of little man
who runs big errands
for the truly big men

& if he keeps his mouth buttoned
may live to retire
as a part-time landshark
in Agent Haven

"The ass waggeth his ears"

Seems like some of these
younger ones grew up
still believing that old
hype about this being
"a *fast* world"

    the world ain't fast

it's big & sluggish & doesn't
give a shit about your microbial jerking around

    widescreen night stars

    smudge planes slow

    astronomical corkscrew aesthetics

as chemically complicated as poetry equals curved speech

"They drove cars fast —
Neon was young —"

(for Tom Raworth)

There was was there not a time
one sallied forth

big provider hunter
irately affectionate
vis-à-vis wife & bairns

(nostalgicly fond in thought
of the bucolic founding friggers

Whereas now
one despondently feels
all that to have been just rotten
rearguard imperialist stuff

Well izzat so
Well tell me it ain't

(enter smiling young neo-imperialist critic
bearing gigantic laurels

The tenth of May (1988)

Jane is out being a delegate
    when she comes home
we'll light the candle & have some spinach spaghetti
with Mr. Paul Newman his sauce
his good cause sauce & smiling face on the label

I do add a dash of Worcestershire
    a little garlic & some white pepper

oh Eros we thank thee for thy gifts
this day the day
    of the great book burnings in Deutschland
        fifty-five years ago

Bright Moments

when it all makes sense
"deciphers"
a great crystal forest
enchanting

terrifying
because it seems only a sneeze away
from incomprehensible chaos
whose lineaments we are

only beginning to
decipher

"whose lineaments
we are"

well you go out there
& then come back in-
to the midst of whatever
awful things

the people who 'make' money
make a *lot* of money
make money off of

but here walks a portly or is it potty? bearded person
carrying shopping bag moving along
up the street in big white sneakers
having descended from stately vintage Checker Cab

it is God
forever unemployed
but really *muy contento*

The endowment

of the W. C. Fields
        College for Boys & Girls

"where no religion
        whatsoever
            will be taught"

he left $800,000
            ($10,000 to wife

& wife & lawyers
        took it all

            thus saving these States
        from generations
            of smart atheists

In the Land of Art

the artists
work on the art farm.

They store the art they make
in the art barn.

Once in a while, they take some out
& take it to the art store.

When the art store sells some,
they take their share
& put it in the art bank.

Then they take their art checkbooks
& go to the art inn
to have a good time.

Or take each other to an art movie
or an art dance.

They wash their clothes at the art laundromat
unless they are successful & rich & have
their own art washer & dryer
in their art basement.

When the artists take a trip
(an art trip)
they stay at the art hotel.

When they get sick, they go to the art hospital.
& when they die, they're buried
in the art cemetery.

& that's the life of the artists
in the land of art.

don't drop the yule log
on your foot

the clock strikes three
can't think of words for this space
(he feels like a louse)

in Point Barrow, Alaska
it must be time to go to the bar
but we're not there
(nor in bars much anymore

these
do not seem like the right words

The ocean of savage lusts
in which the wounded shark
gnashes
at his own tail
is not our home
— William Carlos Williams to José Garcia Villa

Shut up!
I don't feel good!
— tall bearded man, wild eyes
wearing blue sleeping bag down the street
arguing with his anima
or mama, more likely

a small herd of medical personnel
may or may not catch up with him later
(the case, no doubt
with all of us

It is the seed that floats ashore
one word, one tiny, even microscopic word
which can alone save us

where is it, where is it

do send it along if you see it

Professional Armaments

— for Carl Rakosi, who wrote "OK"

December 5, 1988: the phone rings to inform me, in the voice of a male fellow human, that there is a package addressed to myself but to the wrong address, consisting of two books in the Swedish language, at the premises of an enterprise called *Professional Armaments* in the township of Murray, Utah. Could I come and pick it up? Sure, I say, but couldn't you just re-address it to me here in nearby Salt Lake City? The voice indicates strong doubts as to the feasibility of this, so I drive some miles in foggy weather and arrive at *Professional Armaments*.

It is a large, brightly lit store crammed to the rafters with weaponry, enough to outfit a small army: there are cases, shelves, and wall displays of handguns, assault rifles, machine guns, rocket launchers, stun guns, tear gas canisters, handcuffs, leg irons, truncheons, knives, bulletproof armor, you name it. Two soberly garbed gentlemen stand at the other end of the counter discussing the purchase of three dozen infrared nightscopes. A pleasantly schoolmarmish female employee hands me my package.

Back in the car I discover that the grievously misaddressed books are autobiographical works by my friend Mia Berner, the widow of fellow poet Pentti Saarikoski (see "Bro Hipponax," page 29, for his posthumous communication), whose *Tiarnia Trilogy* I have just finished translating. Mia's books deal with her childhood and youth in the late Thirties and early Forties; the second volume concludes with a scene in which she, a teenage girl, is rowing a boat carrying, besides her, two heavily armed plainclothes policemen, Norwegian collaborators with the Nazi occupation forces, and her lover, whom these agents have arrested at an island hideout and are now taking into custody. She tells one of them to stop gesticulating with his carbine — the barrel is getting in the way of her rowing.

24

On the occasion of & as
an introduction to
Robert Creeley's reading at
Kulttuuritalo ("The House of
Culture") in Helsinki, Finland
on Valentine's Day '89

time & again when I falter & half believe
those always articulate dogmatics
who say our words can never be our own

but are merely signs
devised by controllers
(the controllers being the other dogmatics
on top of the heap)

thus
they say
anything one might say
is merely a reflection
of those historico-socio-economic conditions
that make one this deluded
miserable
little pile of shit

that presumes to have thoughts
feelings
epiphanies *recognitions*
of use to others as species fellows

I think of the way a hawk's
or a gopher's days are an investigation
of its world

the way the days & words

of Robert Creeley's poems are
an investigation
of our human universe

se on saatanan hyvä runoilija
se panee psyyken lepattelemaan

a bloody great poet / he makes the psyche flutter

like the little white curtain
in the candle-lit window
at the end of the booby-trapped garden path

"and Today's Credo is ..."

Don't feel like hiding in the archetypes

Don't trust the stuff that's supposed to give you
      The Grand Shivers
(take top off head, etc.

But what about melodious?

Melodious
I have trouble with

So I guess this avuncular
vernacular
will have to do

Too much money or was it honey

The decadent aesthete deals brilliantly with the disgusting
but the brilliant decadent
 then deals disgustingly with the aesthete

They're both in line for The Farting Rosebush Award
and they are, both of them, you

Bro Hipponax / *an inscription:*
Pentti Saarikoski / 1937 – 1983

WHEN I WAS EIGHTEEN
I WROTE BETTER POEMS
THAN DID YOU
WHEN YOU WERE EIGHTEEN

NOW, IN OUR FIFTIES,
I AM DEAD
& YOU
MUST GO ON WRITING
AS BEST YOU CAN

29

Tarp / *for Kit Robinson*

Warm & soft
or cold & hard

the taco of existence
lies in front of the bard

who remembers
here in the dark

the barf on your shoes
shaped like a backwards question mark

& as you blink off
the snow keeps falling

over The Searchers
& their dim expectations

In the "hip" little bookshop

catering to the local
writing workshop's needs & tastes
(works by the faculty
& their friends

predictable stylish "fiction"
predictable stylish "poems"

I mutter to myself "but this is
just shit, it looks like books
but it's just shit"

I feel embarrassed
but I don't wake up

it isn't just a bad dream

but out in the street
in the front yards
there are these hyacinths
& daffodils

goddamn little crowd pleasers

Lord Lytton Goes to
Language School

"I write for exertion in proud minds. I am, it is true, generally, and think without object. Reputed clever, fools are afraid as I actively interfere with thinking. It is necessary to block head. My mind is legitimate in its destiny of exertion. I began severe thought: what was once put must be connected with paper. Days pass. Ideas become myself, the likeness of rapidity fused with method. A week. No object but intellectual want, overcharged like most writings of the thick and confused. I turn into a Dalmatian."

"It was all about . . ."

poor communications

mistaken identity

voyages   battles   sieges & potions

returns

black sails

& dying

in love

after a busy life

Or, What I Remember of Tristan & Isolde

Cricket Poetics /
for Kaarina Hollo

"Here   here"
the crickets again

the real thing not young Kevin's
hi-tech alarm clock
in the trunk of our car

in the Moab desert
strongly proposed
(by myself)
as mysterious
Desert Cricket

well   investigation
oftentimes proves us wrong

but "here   here"
an invisible legion

& that's what we are
the poets

an invisible legion

almost as audible

sometimes

who wrote this

being a poet these days is a little like
playing the harmonica
                    —John Chamberlain

when we were little poets
we told ourselves
one day
we'll have a big book
just like the big poets

& now
we have big books
but are we big poets now
don't make me laugh ha ha

though even Charles Olson
has not been the same
since the academics ate him

o I do not wish to remember
have trouble recalling
find it hard to believe

what a day it was
flags were flying
bands were playing
& all the lovely ladies
had flowers in their hair

(& that was first written
by Munro Leaf
author of *Ferdinand the Bull*
a great poem

Wordsworth briefly revisited

do you behold these steep & lofty cliffs
with huge & black projection overbrowed
as fall upon us often when we look
amid the heart of many thousand mists

that hulk which labors in the deadly swell
within the sonnet's scanty plot of ground
& all its aching joys are now no more
as slips the book from hand to floor

In the library of poets' recordings

the dead speakers
we can hear
but the dead listeners
can not be retrieved

ah yes

The time I thought I heard a master tell me
that there was "a lot of cunt" in my poems

& felt a little flustered & flattered or maybe not or both

then realized he'd said "a lot of *fun*"

Letter to Uncle O. / *for Andrei Codrescu*

Dear Publius Ovidius
    "The Nose"
missing ah missing the rose
    of Rome
for ten years of letters in verse

in one of them, startled to find yourself
    calling drear Tomis "home"
— a shantytown by the frozen Black Sea
    where people grow fur & look daggers

& no spreak-a-da Latin
    but something called Getic
Getic! or at best broken Greek
    & winter is a year long

while you pen song upon song
    to send
where you once were young
    listing your poet friends by name
& even some whose names you can't recall

praising that lovely sodality
    of once-upon-a-time
a welcome break for your reader
    who's 2,000 years too late

to do a thing about the ostensible reason
    for your lengthy *Tristia* or *Drearies:*
the Emperor's pardon

because that emperor lives
    only within the rose
        of a city more perennial

where dream & memory converse
    carouse & conjure
        breathlessly deathless

(& who could pardon himself that way
    except now & again
        between the lines

the missing page

It was a poem, the jittery sort

"about" struggling through rush hour
traffic in downtown Baltimore

then, seeing you

there, on the far side of the river

of steel & plastic & sentient bags of water

cloaked & hatted   smiling

perhaps in disbelief at seeing me pass
the second time, in midstream, unable
to pull ashore to let you embark

(it also had some quote from a Godard
—just clumsy artifice)

The thing, the thing was

"how do you say?" immense

                    yearning & delight

clearly & dearly / *for JDH, 15:X:88*

"gone wrong"
so many ways
    (not heeding parental
    or much of any other
        advice

a determined
    irregular
        in the navies of utterance
    no rank no commission
follower of admirals Loser & Loser
        in the literary campaigns)

I feel remarkably cheerful
    (considering)
because it is your birthday today

        & we are quite clearly afloat
    in the uncharted archipelago
        of Being-Here

& because
    having found you
        is clearly & dearly one thing
            I done right

Response to Colorado Daily's
poll question: "What is
the meaning of life?"

life is a leaf
stuck to her nose
very brief-
ly, just a mo

idyll

water
the yard o
wild domestic

Alla Petrarca

Downtown
Madison, Wisconsin at night
is pretty quiet. Returning

from the dinner for scholars of Finnish
in black plastic boots that seem to be shrinking
I listen to their heels on the sidewalk and feel like

a German Romantic
a hundred and fifty years younger, enveloped
in my sense of missing you, oh fairest of ladies!

back home in Boulder,
Colorado. It is storybook time, as when we saw
that gown in the window in Stockholm Old Town

yesterday? Or the day before?
We who are of this gender, what can we do —
we know it must be a burden to you

to appear in our visions as the *summum bonum*
the great female sun our souls do yearn for
but at least you don't have to do it in person

every time. My feet hurt but I am so glad

       (receding footsteps)

chansons d'antan

Greenery waves in wind
o eerie
             underwater light

        et les chansons d'antan

weave of keyboard & saw & Bromige
             says the marimba
makes them stagger *un peu*
             on the wide curving steps
             (the men
of a certain age

my son my son why hast thou forsaken the world

two oranges in a silver bowl

             & if the dinosaurs
             "became birds"
             what will we "become"

SO

— in memoriam
Kalevi Lappalainen (1940 — 1988)

a lifetime ago
we sat in small
Helsinki café

('Dutch genre dark'
as I remember)

discussing the translation
of then current idioms

the term "high"
in particular

as in "boy am I ever high"
or "it's a good high"
or just "to be high"

& you came up with
"to be up on a branch"

we giggled
two cartoon birdies
up on our little branch

then went back to our chosen lands

& now
it really is
a lifetime gone

& how would you translate that

La Mort

probably
another
of those appointments
one keeps putting off

knowing
one has to keep them
one day

"If I
refuse to go
to the dentist

maybe I won't
have to die"

nice curly hair

It come to the Pope
& to the nightcrawler too

death
is shit

equals loose molecules
(whether it's violins or grenades)

but & I quote the distinctive charm
of YZ's poems

resides in their unselfconscious mastery
of universal late 20th century modes

unquote informed
by her warm young life

so
Fuck Death

is what one must say at all points
of one's silly little existence right?

right right
do not go gentle into that *buenas noches*

in Tashkent or Nacogdoches
wherever whoever you are make a fuss

a Big Fuss
before the Big Foot comes down

Jeremiah Digest

hair falls off head
head falls off body

nothing new under the sun

but evolution
must have slowed
to a *crawl*

old love
or war
poem

I
  know
      where
         you are!
I
  can
    see the
       bushes
         moving!

"Sales figures are up"
(for Robert Grenier)

i.e., there're more of these human
figures
up & about & paying for things
by making more things to buy

strafed
the curb

while turning into the parking
lot with a head cold & sadness
en mi corazón

due to word of two
true friends who were also lovers
living together for many years

but now are an item no more no more
so there are more of us
than ever before

but two
people imagined happy together
less

& I meant to say "bumped"
"bumped the curb"

but I said *strafed*
didn' I

sonnet

Morning strides through these poems
be they turds of protest or histories of the alphabet
social symbolic or just produce
metaphysical grovel   stirrings in the eaves

old baboons at work on our investigations i.e.
"curving rhythmical accidents which loop
        into old choral & liturgical songs
into certain kinds of modern music
even into tunes from banal popular song"

that was Leonardo   Leonardo Sinisgalli speaking

we speak together   then we say
"I always quite misunderstood you"

how grotesque this world
even without us

just two guys struggling with a big sheet
on the stony side of the street

no detachment

Step out   snow and sunshine
walking   feels good
two blocks   bank machine
working!   good
on to local market
salad stuff   good
head back   small detour
bookshop   browse   my books still there
good   or bad   not sold   buy
last Sunday's New York Times Book Review
more Joyce Carol Oates   oh well
all right   stop   red light
plastic shopping bag on left wrist
shake wrist a little   make sure
watch still on   back home
tuna snack shared with cats   good
sudden good god! realization
watch is gone

retrace steps   look everywhere
house   street   call bookshop
wretched day   watch gone
nice watch gone   rage   confusion   dry
tears   mutter mutter   what's the use
snow   sunshine   life is shit
Roman numerals   lovely
picked out with Jane Dalrymple
me protesting excessive elegance   expense
growl sigh yes
                    an evil iguana tongue
flashed out of the Void today

"He the old guy"

he sure enjoys this cutlery he used to eat with as a kid
aahh, yes
"Chimborazo, Cotopaxi"
carried him away

& it seems only yesterday
into the arms of a wondrous wise woman
where he purrs & chortles
like Caligula in his finest moments

he used to be a shortwave broadcaster in London
but now
he is a star surfer in Salt Lake City Utah
& like Caligula & Christ

(as shamelessly subjective)
he too will be gone one day
at crocus time
in some part of the universe

aahh, yess
but he does like
these imitation bone handles
& the Zeppelin Era spikiness of the forks

la vida / *para Janey, mi vida*

Through swirls & eddies of footfalls
converging, diverging

some soft, some percussive
she walks to work

thinks of the two
happy young people

glimpsed in the car behind her
& how they *glowed*

among thousands streaming along in their shells
under big plumes of dark smoke under heaven

later says "If I wrote poems
those are things I would write about"

& I say, well, that — that's a *movie* —
but later think, no

it isn't, it's *life*
It's life, all right

Brother (D. H.) Lawrence

& all the eerie
'previous' states of mind

in which one was rushing
around inside

of a roughly
spherical tangle of self-
generated messages

& turned up high, for sure,
to the point of despair

ah, the *drama* of it all!

which was exactly what Brother
Lawrence had warned one against

but better reception
came only much later

such as the one
one is enjoying

this radio morning —
his birthday: a hundred and three —

with Ellen Burstyn, an actress
reading his number on The Turtle

Glenwood Springs

Under Doc Holliday's
weary eyes

      last scanned
just before Checkout Time
in that fake Vienna hotel

my lady, rising
                  out of steam
(but not at all
"out of steam"

straight, lovely
            as mountains

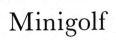

Minigolf

In the Spring of '88, Anselm and Jane
played a round of miniature golf
somewhere between New
Orleans and Biloxi. Anselm
kept the scorecard and named poems
written during the remainder of the year
after each obstacle on the course —
thus, *Minigolf,* sporadically
annotated, became a kind of record of
the Game of that Year.

The Way

The way you got to be the way you were
just a moment ago

is the way of "the moment"
a big old notion in which you can never

find yourself
so stagger on on your quest

for the other big old notion
"the now"

as in *right now*
as you just were right then

Castle

"These be the spears that our imperium braved" points at

wrought-iron fence symbolic reminder of assegais dense

in the air of (his) head supported by feet (his) on

American lawn modeled on those of an England there

Pinball

Woke up & was being
a nice human being again

baffled but cheerful among the other
480,000 non-Mormons

in this administrative space

& once again quite able
to sit around the old oaken table

the dinner was cooked to perfection

the bang
will follow the flash

yes nukes
have indeed led to a worldwide upsurge

of mad religiosity
don't you think blink think

Alligator

To live there
in Baton Rouge

one of the globe's
greatest concentrations

of massive
man-made
pollution

takes *guts!*
big guts!
big *reptilian* guts!

"He wrote that
because he didn't get the job"

Who said that?! — I'll — I'll — @#*!!#@**!!! —

Elephant

Ted Berrigan says this to you:

"We are each free to shed big crystal tears on
The dirt-covered ground, tied together only
By white clouds and some mud we can find, if we try,
In the darksome orange shadows of the big blue swamp"

He says this to you in his forty-seventh sonnet on page 47
of his great book THE SONNETS

Which you'd do well to read at least once a week here

"on the vast salt deserts of America
Where Snow White sleeps among the silent dwarfs"

Boy, this one was easy.
But, "how long can a quote get, he sd, eyeing me…"
Now locate *that* quote.

Pygmy Hut

Heavy drops
fell from the trees
& made a
plopping
sound
as they hit
the poodles

(shouldn't that be 'puddles'

(no
not puddles
poodles

Heavy drops
fell from the trees
& made a
plopping
sound
as they hit
the poodles

This is sort of a French poem.
It has, how do you say, *l'espace.*

Around The World

My first introduction
to the "Valentine" concept

was an American animated cartoon
preceding a Hopalong Cassidy movie

I'd dragged my mother to in Stockholm
in 1943 or 4

Valentine's Day
is a bit like May Day in Red Square

both are celebrations of cherished ideas
but considering

their flawed realizations
over time
the celebrations seem a little overdone

Hills

Don't just sit there she said
like a lumpy fog

feeling lonely & sorry for
some imagined self

There's no need to feel lonely
there's lots of people out there

Yes I know he said but I'm still lonely
for my friends
my *dead* friends

Oh come on she said

you're just indulging in the midway crankies
past-midlife lumpies & grumpies

come on let's go climb some *hills*

The Jump

Drive to the Beef & Bourbon
in Bowling Green Ohio

with Andrew Carrigan & Tom Raworth
in nineteen seventy-something

have a T-bone steak
have a couple of beers & six shots of bourbon

then jump back to the present
(nineteen eighty-something)

grinning & shaking your head
pleased that we're all still alive

(as of the date of this writing)

Rocket

Teacher, teacher
— I don't like this assignment

I never liked rockets
& the one on the minigolf course
somewhere between New Orleans & Biloxi
where all this started
wasn't going anywhere anyway

& that evening felt definitely pre-rocket
at least the way we think of them now
(to do with Buck Rogers or nuclear wipeout)

much more like balloon
post-chaise & brigantine

Kinder & gentler,
like no CIA?

Glance

it,
there

The managers of this establishment
have come here from another part of the universe

their cooking smells good so never mind the incense
slightly too sweet

wafting into the lobby from the room
behind the reception desk

where they conduct their private lives
(now would this be greater 'in meter'?

no it wouldn't)
at the local joke shop

we purchase some joke beach towels
to go to the beach

which is a joke
— thin sheets of water stretching for miles

then we hear thunder see lightning no joke!
& retire

to our private lives
back at the inn

they do intertwine
as we do

it,
there

Somewhere between New Orleans & Biloxi

Champ

so it all goes back to some big goofy guy

 holding forth on the universe

in a lit-from-within

transparent

cube of the past

yeah

that's right

Something Norse-Tibetan about this one. *Lineage.*

Lighthouse

The house
in North Platte, Nebraska
is not a lighthouse.

This house
is dark. The curtains are drawn.
Colonel Cody's
not at home.

They're not expecting him back
anytime soon.

Adieux sentimentaux to my childhood's hero,
now immortalized on a postcard stamp.

The Curve

missed
due to alcohol it was
still there
on the other side of the ditch

Somewhere between Marshall and Cottonwood, Minnesota.
Far as I know, it's still there.

Snail

Ess Enn A Eye Ell.
Snail.

Ee Vee Oh Ell You Tee Eye Oh Enn.
Evolution.

Snail
Evolution.

Tic-Toc

or,
lowercase
on joel
& roy

thought he looked a bit jerky
sounded a little too sweet

that evening
at the folk song society
near primrose hill

a young american singer
in red shirt & jeans
i was young too
& had a young son

& all of us in that room went on
to all we went on to
on this orb

in my case even to liking
roy orbison's songs
"pretty woman"
in particular

it being a very particular
song about a
very general
idea

one also much entertained
by the late great american poet
joel oppenheimer
whose "dutiful son"
i was reading then

ave atque vale

Chicken Coop

it's winter he's feeling mean she's tired

he makes a crack about her command of geography

she pretends to stab his wrist with a fork

he brings his fork down hard

 on her plate of Rasta-style beans

both

burst into tears

Strind-
berg.

Berg-
man.

Ragna-
rök, etc.

Nordic Angst.
Weird Genes.

The Fish

in the tank
on the plate
in the mammals' mouths

at 2 a.m.
in Japantown, San Francisco
was

dazzling
quite tasty
kept them awake & talking some more

Present: Jane Dalrymple; Lynne Wildey; Robert Grenier;
Kush; an interesting fellow who talked a lot but whose name the
author can't remember; the author

The Dada Letter

One afternoon in northern Europe, probably in the year 1939, a boychild one now sees wearing a blue velvet Little Lord Fauntleroy suit with lace collar and cuffs, is walking down a chiaroscuro corridor in a haut-bourgeois six-story apartment building —

What Dadaists are still alive are dealing with their life-movies in various ways, suggested by other labels:

Surrealism

Socialism

Psychoanalysisism

within the increasingly hallucinatory public film, Herr Adolf Hitler's "millennial epic" BOY FROM AUSTRIAN BOONIES MAKES GOOD —

The boychild's parents, who met in the Twenties in the capital of the former Austro-Hungarian Empire, never were Dadaists, although they did have the works of Hugo Ball on their shelves —

There really had been no Viennese Dada, the way there was a

Berlin Dada a

Zurich Dada a

Cologne Dada a

Paris Dada a

New York Dada and a

Hannover MERZ —

Vienna and London had their Neo-Dadas many years later, after another World War, and the boychild would have some first-hand experience of those —

Speaking of hands, that boychild (one afternoon probably in 1939) is, in his right hand, carrying a glass plate with a doughnut on it —

When one says "doughnut" here, one is referring to the European kind without a hole, just a ball of fried dough covered in refined white sugar, known in some Teuton-speaking lands as a "Berliner" — whence the essentially Dadaist delight of the inhabitants of Berlin at a Post-Dada United States President's enthusiastic confession that he, too, was just a ball of fried white dough —

This, too, was later — now in '39, the boychild's left hand is most likely engaged in picking his nose or trying to detach the pretty lace collar from his Little Lord Fauntleroy suit —

*

Young Post-Dada Krissie from next door just called to say that there is an Amnesty International special on Channel 2, on women prisoners of conscience — she is a member of Amnesty International, as are Jane and I, and a mover and shaker in the local (Salt Lake City) high school cadres of that organization — a bright sweet blonde young thing who reminds me of my daughters at her age — and *that* seems like an eternity ago — her fellow Amnestyites, on the other hand, affect Modified Punk, that Post- or Neo-Dada marriage of S & M Biker Chic with Seven Nations tonsorial fashions, first consummated in London — where those daughters were born, in the era of Love and Beatles —

I tell her that it is good of her to point this out but that we don't have a television set, as both Jane and I are somewhat afraid of having attention spans totally destroyed and adrenalin levels artificially but permanently raised by daily exposure to that 'medium of the day' — she says that I'm welcome to come over and watch the program on women prisoners of conscience, or prisoners of conscience who are also women — and then I have to tell her thank you but I am at this very moment struggling to get some kind of fix on this lecture I am supposed to give at the Jack Kerouac School of Disembodied Poetics in Boulder, Colorado, in about two weeks' time, on

Dada

Neo-Dada

and Post-Dada — ridiculous idea, I say, isn't it — don't know what possessed me, it wasn't the money — and am tempted to quote the pertinent line from Allen Ginsberg's still-reverberating HOWL: "who threw potato salad at CCNY lecturers on Dadaism" — but don't — but say that maybe she can tell me later about the program — then feel like a prick, sigh, and return to the keyboard of composition to stare at the words "pretty lace collar of his Little Lord Fauntleroy suit" —

I notice that I have typed "worlds" instead of "words" — this makes me think of Gertrude Stein, without a doubt *the* great Dadaist in the American language — I need to quote a poem of hers — but back to that moment one afternoon probably in 1939 when the boychild, walking down a chiaroscuro corridor in a haut-bourgeois six-story apartment building, executes, with his right hand, a gesture somewhat similar to the Fascist salute — one cannot say why but one remembers that he is or now rather was in his right hand carrying a glass plate with a doughnut on it —

When one says "doughnut" here — OK you heard that one already — CUT to Grand Pre-Dada Marcel Proust eating a doughnut —

"now rather was," since the Berliner is now launched on a trajectory through the slightly stale but pleasantly lavender-smelling or is it lily-of-the-valley (the boychild's mother's favorite perfume) air of the corridor —

*

While on a recent expedition to my study or office to get Volume Six of the Yale Edition of the Unpublished Writings of Gertrude Stein, I noted that the indoor temperature had dropped to 79 degrees, thanks to judicious use of the window fan, and also that the radio was playing one of those south-of-the-border classics about living out the Twilight of Empire in a sun-drenched tequila coma — and instantly thought of David Bromige, because of his lines in *Red Hats,* a recent work:

"For those who learned to drink in the 50's, vibraphones will inevitably bring on a slight stagger. Down the steep steps he

slipped with many abrasions, only to find the Club Seren-
dipitee, where caught some GREAT sounds being improv'd
by those cats. Then this chick, see . . ."

— the book *Red Hats* is so tightly bound, "perfect-bound"
I suppose, that I have to type with one hand while the other
holds the book open —

As the doughnut is now flying through that lily-of-the-val-
ley and/or lavender air, the boychild is left holding

      only the glass plate

      which he stops to contemplate

— and how is that for *rime riche* — the doughnut meanwhile
vanishing into the chiaroscuro with what Sir Edward Bul-
wer-Lytton might have described as an inaudible thud —

The Pope just called — he wanted to know if there was any
substance to rumors that his invisible guru — whom he
referred to as Our Lord — would prefer Salt Lake City to
Rome for his Second Coming —

I of course pooh-poohed said rumors and told the dear
Vicar that his boss had told me, at a recent poetry and
rock'n'roll conference in Gothenburg, Sweden, which he
was attending incognito in the guise of a pale and sweating
Finnish blues singer, that he was no longer interested in
religion of the paternalistic sort —

After a brief pause, the pontiff drily remarked that I must
have been reading that dear but over-educated Ernesto
Cardenal again — I said, no no, I had actually been reading
David Bromige, the wonderfully erudite North American
poet and bon-vivant saint of *eiron* —

"The *eiron*, or ironical man, is a man who professes that he
does not have, or has in less measure than the world sup-
poses, the good qualities which he does in fact possess" —

Yes, yes, that's from Aristotle, says the Vicar, a mite
impatiently — well have a nice day, one gathers it is quite hot
out there —

      eiron = *semper dada*

I say well have a good one too — don't let the population
figures get you down —

The doughnut has come to rest in a corner of the corridor —
and the boychild in the blue velvet suit is left holding the glass
plate — momentarily at a loss as to what should be his further
course of action — possibly even *right* action, a concept that's
been looming on his psychic horizon for some time now,
being often discussed by his parents — who have Hugo Ball's
works on their shelf —

Hugo Ball, saint of Zurich Dada, and later ascetic mystic —

who performed his *sound poems* in a costume made out of
big cardboard tubes — looking a bit like the Pope drawn by
Wyndham Lewis — spouting things like "jolifanto bambla ô
falli bambla" — and

"hej tatta gôrem

anlogo bung

blago bung" — and also said "spit out *words*, the
dreary, lame, empty language of society" — rousing stuff —
SEMPER DADA! — from Ball's Russian soul brother Velemir
Khlebnikov — to beast-language Post-Dada American
Michael McClure — and yet

one has gone back to replacing the *zaum* words with the
other kind — those shared with the dreary lame empty
language of society — hasn't one — ah, a vast flood of nostal-
gia washed o'er me — as the indoor temperature resumed its
relentless climb — what "one" needed right then was an
ecologically sound air conditioner — and maybe a videotape
of Post-Dada Tom Stoppard's snotty little "Travesties" —
T. Tzara's and V. I. Lenin's café chess playing days in
Zurich —

on the other hand, this would have set one back an hour
or two in the task of composing the lecture one had in some
weak moment consented to give — to this really hip audience
of fellow poets just about ready to launch the potato salad —

one paused briefly to correct the spelling of "doughnut" by
means of "Word Search and Change," a "feature" of one's
writing implement — ah, there — one is now old enough to
comfortably enjoy being a little old-fashioned —

then one is captivated by the thought that one could change the word "doughnut" to let's see, how about "Stinger missile" —

"as the Stinger missile is now flying through that lily-of-the-valley air" — well it probably is, somewhere on this semper dada globe —

where was one —

"the doughnut has come to rest

some corner of blue velvet hall

in his left the glass a loss

expatiating parents loom" — yes, the old *scramble* — proto-L = A = N = G = U = A = G = E strategy — how one wrote some of one's poems in 1969 Neo-Dada Iowa City — in the good company — semper dada! amigos Actualistas! — even though twenty years later, it is still "venceremos" only in the future tense — vis-à-vis or should one say versus The Big Smirk —

ô jolifanto bambla —

one does stare at the words —

*

The word INTERMISSION — written when one got up from the writing of this piece three days ago — at a loss what else to say —

during this grand intermission — when all of us seem at a loss as to what should be the further course of action — "possibly right action" —

during the intermission at the phantom opera that occasionally haunts this city by the dead inland sea —

I go to the "rest room" in my grey CIA suit — then re-emerge into chandelier chatter — thinking, Dada is dead but Opera lives — ah wistful wistful —

smile politely at the one Michael Jackson look-alike — among all the Burl Ives and Deborah Kerr look-alikes — navigating around and saying things —

who is that tall beauty standing there all by herself — my

heart leaps up as I behold — the gentle, intelligent curve of her neck and silver-streaked hair — and know it is Jane — once again thank the gods we're permitted this time — in the great intermission —

in a place where only a few have to disappear before their time — although some of the best have done so — still few, compared to other places one might name — ruled by the grim Anti- or Idi Amin Dada of los desaparecidos — now back to our movie:

having raised his hand in a vehement gesture — who knows why — on his way from the kitchen and mother — who is power — to father in his study (or office) — who is culture —

with the doughnut on the glass plate — perhaps to ward off some phantom of a five-year-old imagination —

and thus having caused the doughnut to disappear from the plate — the boychild of 1939 decides that right action is no longer possible in this particular case — and so —

lets the plate, too, go
into the chiaroscuro —

it is an act of Proto-Dada devil-may-care despair — and is (luckily) found amusing by both mother power and father culture — as power and culture had found amusing the paper wars between Dadas and Surrealists — now amply documented and catalogued — analyzed and deconstructed — by numerous degree candidates in American institutions of well they say learning —

anlogo bung
blago bung —

so, Dad didn't get his doughnut — the plate, miraculously, did not break —

so the boychild grew up and out of those corridors — and once he'd outgrown Buffalo Bill and Jean-Jacques Rousseau — discovered Kurt Schwitters and Marcel Duchamp — the heroes of Dada — and lived through a heady period of Neo-Dada — when it seemed like John Cage and Jasper Johns — to mention but two — would lead the world — into art forever — but no, you can't stop here —

Arcana Gardens

Arcana Gardens

the cat's apprehensive inside her head
'things' are really hopping   a cat

with wings   now that would be a thing
there's this lady now writes her verses

with built-in lacunae   there still remain 'things'
& things to delete

contained in the changing light
moving the frame & things

from room to room I miss you
when you're gone all day

yet when you're home there's times I'm lost again
inside the side
    shows of my head

in this picture we see an oligarch
flying in his recliner

*

the practice of poetry:
doing it when called upon

oh blast this doglike devotion to the US of A
get ready for MacCommunism

the light inside the body
at the end of long flexible tube

I'm so bit-ter . . .
I'm so pret-ty . . .

       go on up
       or off

bluejay on woodpile
first prize: dinner in Des Moines

second prize: two dinners in Des Moines
well I'm heading for the bedding

the old legacy was a bottle of no anxiety
& one of no grief   those made you high for a while

then laid you low
weird white sugar architecture of that church in Buffalo

the blackness of Gothenburg   permanent diaspora
the ideal state

when the mind/body committee decides
a habit has become immoderate   it's a good idea
      to let it go

*

had to invent religion   ideas of karma afterworld etc.
in order to enjoy ever more highly

structured existence? (requires 'security' 'stability'
less general random viciousness)

an epic of prayers   poetry what you read
when you exercise the *skill* of reading

when tired of record of operatic soprano
(on radio) stuck on the two little words *da capo*

the world is bigger than your head   or even mine

*

oh it's just like magazines used to be — with poems
by Ted in them

(who wants them to *like* their poetry
as long as they *read* it)

well it's time to be drizzling on
truckloads of stuff to keep us within the framework

but writers of small language groups
their admirable stubbornness

clings to the 'absoluteness'
of their particular language

their words   by extension that's of course true
of everybody

(don't know if I'll ever feel like writing 'about' the times
in life I was a total idiot asshole?)

"I want a longer attention span"
"he wants a longer dick?"

Finns: some general sense of shaggy folks tough
eking out a precarious   up there up Norf

"my metaphor machine is bigger than yours"
all greed relative?   love work that sails close
        to its own parody

stand up a berserker   end up a beseecher
in the vast stone forest of the world's war memorials

the ghosts of generals stumble about
dishevelled confused   graffiti on the great moving wall

moving toward The Wall   résumés for god
Papa wanted me to marry the Finnish language

Mama   chemistry   (her father's life)
both kept me away from Finnish-speaking women
      with all their might

so I went to Germania & married a German speaker
but couldn't make a living in those countries

so ended up in England   thus changing
my great love affair with the English (specifically
      American)

language into a lifetime commitment/marriage

*

old staples-through-the-side books　　they *work*
people pay more attention to the right-hand page

each text gets equal weight　　maybe the species
(homo sap) doesn't spend enough time

looking at admiring coveting what it eats (anymore)
thought while watching cat watching birds

at feeder on other side of glass　　"he had trouble
announcing a formal presence"　　gazing at red orange
& green

in slowly steaming pan it occurs to me not at all suddenly
that one I grieve for may well be content

to be living completely alone in a universe
of the greatest possible distances

Bertolucci's last emperor of China
a life just like everybody's

the emperor child　　the live-forever young man
the long haul to the end

*

"killed by orthodox reality" (Peter Handke)
a Linnéan classification of poets?

re-reading Corso: *that t*radition   the sixties out of the fifties
so sturdy   later poetry much more nervous

viz. Grenier's frontispiece for Phantom Anthems
Nerve Man   yet in him as in Berrigan

still that cheek
     & glint

when it degenerates into homily exhortation
or some disguise of those (story or antistory with moral)

it loses the power to drive us happily crazy for a minute
or two totally out
     of our gourds for one of those

          eternal moments
     of *le merveilleux*

*

cut to Pearl Street in Boulder where frisky yuppies
& even aging hippies go shopping for earrings

we just have this little bit of the haul to do
the forms formalities with which we 'stave off' death &
        thought of it

the common customary ones   & then the 'deeper' ones
such as some music   some poems

walking in the wild word woods   first reading Corso
say or EP for that matter   that old strut

that old fiddling while Rome burns canto strut

*

weird inverted Puritan desire to prove one's mettle
through suffering   stoically & wittily

behind the idea   of giving readings
drunk stoned on speed mushrooms acid

(handed down by that Welshman   possibly farther back)
like the embarrassed drunk father

only when drunk is he able
to admit non-utilitarian emotion

& LDS part of that mind-boggling Anglo appropriation
of chosen people ism

via King James Bible   also still active in Aryan
Nations types who claim that Anglos

& "Northern Europeans"
are the true descendants of Israel

but the true inhabitants of these deserts & mountains
be lizard coyote   Paiute & Ute & Shoshoni
    (Bear River Massacre)

present-day natives displaying their wounds
(kid in front of Rio Grande Station) & scars

you go out there then you come back in
where the well-meant sentiment meets the hopeful cliché

Hemingway   a bounder & proud of it
the beauty of a genuinely *playful* life

possible?
isn't it?

*

composing from notebooks   a mobile with side shows
"& here we see"   here I see cryptic entry Actual Filth
        "Is that actual filth?"

some poems seem most effortful   as if their author
had labored   over them

ten hours a day seven days a week   & that's
what's wrong with them   "naphthaline"

mothballs of my childhood   naphtha = crude oil
right (check) trudge trudge (glasses in other room etc.)

o be *glad !* you have
many rooms to walk

instead of having to write all your poems in another life at
Mutant State University   "your own medicine"

my mother used to say   "just you wait until *you*
have children" etc.

really just a young 23-year-old American poet (came here
        in '66)
or should we start with '51   London   38 in that case

        & here we see
        the analytical
        bent

*

Orff's Carmina Burana quite lovely but also quite like
a bunch of young Nazis roaring

well I can't do everything at once
bet you could if you tried

yelling at each other in front of the computer
the sublime just fell asleep & died

but the utter & certainly quite wonderful *craziness*
of 'analytical language' (Situationist texts

Derrida Heidegger before them for sure) such gorgeous
kudzu lingo   dog noise pollution

"I hope you're not *confusing* the computer"
was it an hour ago I sat there in London wondering

about Ted Berrigan   this tough young American poet &
critic in the pages of KULCHUR magazine

"the testament of beauty" & what was that all about
well I'm sure it had its share of dog noise pollution

a little vulgar eloquence   yes lowercase american
is what I am   a big invisible fish
      on a chops *gig*

"like playing for eight hours a day at Disneyland"
so little has been written about x

because x's work cannot be paraphrased   this
is the goal of all poetry   it is indeed

impossible to ascertain what x is really writing about or
      rather
it is that x rarely writes about

but is a manifestation
on the page
                  in the air

dance of dada   dance of death
it only writes itself little by little

a walk through the desert of many faces
by the fountain of six patina'd frogs

the houseboy was told off for sweeping *around*
the outside doormats   in the city of New Or*leens*

let's only be classified when dead
& then perhaps resumed
        in Spanish dark

& if a little myth comes with the territory
that's always nice   & cleanly temporal

human rights day? the day no government's able
to raise an army

for quite some time the way was to fall in love
& you can put quotes around all of the above

over & over
                hi ho hi ho

child's (my) vision of work as somehow
martially? pleasurable

being a poet gives one permission to be a crank & even
a crank in print

but you   my species
you're trying to overwhelm the planet
        by numbers?

*

hooked on English   I make six cents a word
no epiphany sans community

the dick came striding down the hall
"goddamn fucking greek deities again"

old Mozart . . . young Cassandra . . . owls
swoop through the canyon at night

aah   am I supposed to say aah?   is this
the 'aah experience'?

who you asking?   dunno
is Robt. Bly around?

we pay the state to kill all those we'd rather not think about
but "a real house with stairs & everything"

you deserve it dear daughter
far more than all the bigdick religious entrepreneurs

who've stuck together
across the centuries

    Sam's Bar & Mosque
        (a hypothetical place)

*

living like happy savages with no t.v.   Arcana Gardens
& he's fifty-five   my goodness   let's dangle on
            down the street

poetry bookshelves   dear elephant graveyard
Science & Democracy

"even just *thinking* about it
ups your production of benign neuropeptides"

all the words this critter can say
when awed by all the worlds   up there

Cygnus XI HDE 22 68 68
Black Jewel of the Northern Cross   down here

DIAMONDS GUNS TV'S   in the Pavlovian pawn shop
string 'em out

them colored lights
then turn 'em off again

            *

up on into what's this all about
this critter makes up its own rules

at the speed
of greed

last night my love got up out of bed & banged
her head on the doorjamb

this evening there's a report on UFO sightings in
Guatemala & it's been very
    windy
        all day

*

ah Babylon I exalt thee above thy detractors
Babylon is The Old Days   The Babylon All Stars

jazz in the ruins
before the ruins

"hey man I just walked out in my slippers"
when I say I wrote that   it is my intention to state

that someone using this same body did write that
then   yes here we see him

his brain   made that metaphor
mid rock & fern adream   with Chingachgook & Cody

but that man in Angola
said to have killed two priests for criticizing his poems

    boy
        that man must write
    some Satanic Verses

*

Colonel Walden at Pulkovo   lauded by Lenin
in John Reed's *Ten Days that Shook the World*

heard on tape on the way to Taos
"HEY THAT'S MY GRAND-UNCLE"

don't burn that flag
boil it & eat it with hot sauce

because I had spent 35 minutes in the bookstore
I felt I had to pay 6.50 for this magazine

I didn't really need then walked on
in the rain past more people resting

dying or dead on the sidewalk
Die Welt frisst was der Fall ist

(the world eats what falls down)
give the homeless $45,000 per capita

& make them *sole* subject of *all* U.S. news for a year
& let every township in the U.S.

have a simulated four-year oil boom
in alphabetical order

with acid trips among
        the gnomes

*

on the sidewalk a large
dog turd shaped like the male
    procreative organ

"none shall be permitted to retain their shape"
well sir you may be right   Roxie Powell of Baltimore

calls in the early a.m. he's working on a novel
whose heroes are Appearance & Reality

more power to him he did insist we go find you my love
down in the bookbinder's Hades (climate controlled)

for the rest of the story   see page

*

see page   & then see page
page after page
as it goes along

until "one day" it stops
with a squeal or a pop   but for now let's go on

to sing the praises of a brown-eyed girl
"I met in a country town"
                             & love
as light & filigreed but also mud-heavy
       as the old songs

with our glasses slightly askew on our noses

     "time for your Van Morrison sir"